ENCOURAGEMENT
Scripture for Daily Living

ENCOURAGEMENT

Scripture for Daily Living

Copyright © 1990 Antioch Publishing Company
Yellow Springs, Ohio 45387
ISBN 0-89954-509-2

CONTENTS

Sharing

Serving

Daily Living

FRIENDSHIP

A friend loves at all times...

Proverbs 17:17

Two are better than one, because...
if one falls down, his friend can
help him up.

Ecclesiastes 4:9,10

...the pleasantness of one's friend
springs from his earnest counsel.

Proverbs 27:9

I am a friend to all...who follow
Your precepts.

Psalm 119:63

"Greater love has no one than this,
that one lay down his life for his
friends."

John 15:13

But if we walk in the light, as He is in the light, we have fellowship with one another...

1 John 1:7

GIVING TO OTHERS

A generous man will himself be blessed...

Proverbs 22:9

"Give to the one who asks you, and do not turn away from the one who wants to borrow from you."

Matthew 5:42

"But when you give to the needy, do not let your left hand know what your right hand is doing, so that your giving may be in secret. Then your Father, Who sees what is done in secret, will reward you."

Matthew 6:3,4

"Freely you have received, freely give."

Matthew 10:8

"It is more blessed to give than to receive."

Acts 20:35

Share with God's people who are in need.

Romans 12:13

Whoever sows sparingly will also reap sparingly, and whoever sows generously will also reap generously.

2 Corinthians 9:6

Each man should give what he has decided in his heart to give, not relunctantly or under compulsion, for God loves a cheerful giver.

2 Corinthians 9:7

Because of the service by which you have proved yourselves, men will praise God...for your generosity in sharing with them and with everyone else.

2 Corinthians 9:13

Command them to do good, to be rich in good deeds, and to be generous and willing to share. In this way they...may take hold of the life that is truly life.

1 Timothy 6:18,19

LEADERSHIP

"So give Your servant a discerning heart to govern Your people and to distinguish between right and wrong. For who is able to govern this great people of Yours?"

1 Kings 3:9

"In the same way, let your light shine before men, that they may see your good deeds and praise your Father in heaven."

Matthew 5:16

Let my teaching fall like rain and my words descend like dew, like showers on new grass, like abundant rain on tender plants.

Deuteronomy 32:2

"Therefore go and make disciples of all nations...teaching them to obey everything I have commanded you."

Matthew 28:19,20

In everything set them an example by doing what is good. In your teaching show integrity, seriousness and soundness of speech...

Titus 2:7

We have different gifts, according to the grace given us...if it is leadership, let him govern diligently...

Romans 12:6,8

MARRIAGE

He who finds a wife finds what is good
and receives favor from the Lord.

Proverbs 18:22

"So they are no longer two, but one.
Therefore what God has joined together,
let man not separate."

Matthew 19:6

Marriage should be honored by all...

Hebrews 13:4

Many waters cannot quench love;
rivers cannot wash it away.

Song of Songs 8:7

...each one of you also must love his wife
as he loves himself, and the wife must
respect her husband.

Ephesians 5:33

Love is patient, love is kind...
Love never fails.

1 Corinthians 13:4,8

The husband should fulfill his marital duty to his wife, and likewise the wife to her husband.

1 Corinthians 7:3

FAMILY

"But as for me and my household, we
will serve the Lord."

Joshua 24:15

...the whole family was filled with
joy, because they had come to believe
in God.

Acts 16:34

...if we love each other, God lives in us
and His love is made complete in us.

1 John 4:12

Be kind and compassionate to one another, forgiving each other, just as in Christ God forgave you.

Ephesians 4:32

Children's children are a crown to the aged, and parents are the pride of their children.

Proverbs 17:6

"Believe in the Lord Jesus, and you will be saved—you and your household."

Acts 16:31

RAISING CHILDREN

Train a child in the way he should go, and
when he is old he will not turn from it.

Proverbs 22:6

"Let the little children come to Me,
and do not hinder them, for the kingdom
of heaven belongs to such as these."

Matthew 19:14

...do not exasperate your children;
instead, bring them up in the
training and instruction of the Lord.

Ephesians 6:4

"...whoever welcomes a little child
like this in My name welcomes Me."

Matthew 18:5

These commandments that I give you today are to be upon your hearts. Impress them on your children.

Deuteronomy 6:6,7

MOTHERHOOD

Her children arise and call her blessed...

Proverbs 31:28

"Many women do noble things, but
you surpass them all."

Proverbs 31:29

"Whoever welcomes this little
child in My name welcomes Me..."

Luke 9:48

Give her the reward she has earned,
and let her works bring her praise...

Proverbs 31:31

May the Lord bless you...and may you live to see your children's children.

Psalm 128:5,6

She speaks with wisdom, and faithful instruction is on her tongue.

Proverbs 31:26

But His mother treasured all these things in her heart.

Luke 2:51

DOING GOD'S WILL

"Walk in the way that the Lord your God has commanded you..."

Deuteronomy 5:33

"Submit to God and be at peace with Him; in this way prosperity will come to you."

Job 22:21

Blessed are they whose ways are blameless, who walk according to the law of the Lord. Blessed are they who keep His statutes and seek Him with all their heart. They do nothing wrong; they walk in His ways.

Psalm 119:1-3

Teach me to do Your will, for You are my God...

Psalm 143:10

But if anyone obeys His word, God's love is truly made complete in Him.

1 John 2:5

Jesus replied, "If anyone loves Me, he will obey My teaching. My Father will love him, and We will come to him and make Our home with him."

John 14:23

"If you obey my commands, you will remain in My love, just as I have obeyed My Father's commands and remain in His love."

John 15:10

This is love for God: to obey His commands. And His commands are not burdensome, for everyone born of God overcomes the world.

1 John 5:3,4

"If only you had paid attention to My commands, your peace would have been like a river, your righteousness like the waves of the sea."

Isaiah 48:18

SERVING GOD

"But as for me and my household, we will serve the Lord."

Joshua 24:15

Commit to the Lord whatever you do, and your plans will succeed.

Proverbs 16:3

"For it is written: 'Worship the Lord your God, and serve Him only.' "

Matthew 4:10

It is the Lord your God you must follow, and Him you must revere. Keep His commands and obey Him; serve Him and hold fast to Him.

Deuteronomy 13:4

"But be very careful...to love the Lord your God, to walk in all His ways, to obey His commands, to hold fast to Him and to serve Him with all your heart and all your soul."

Joshua 22:5

There are different kinds of service, but the same Lord. There are different kinds of working, but the same God works all of them in all men.

1 Corinthians 12:5,6

...faith by itself, if it is not accompanied by action, is dead.

James 2:17

...serve Him with wholehearted devotion and with a willing mind, for the Lord searches every heart and understands every motive behind the thoughts. If you seek Him, He will be found by you...

1 Chronicles 28:9

Serve the Lord with gladness; come before Him with joyful songs.

Psalm 100:2

"No one can serve two masters. Either he will hate the one and love the other, or he will be devoted to the one and despise the other. You cannot serve both God and Money."

Matthew 6:24

But now, by dying to what once bound us, we have been released from the law so that we serve in the new way of the Spirit, and not in the old way of the written code.

Romans 7:6

Never be lacking in zeal, but keep your spiritual fervor, serving the Lord.

Romans 12:11

Always give yourselves fully to the work of the Lord, because you know that your labor in the Lord is not in vain.

1 Corinthians 15:58

Whatever you do, work at it with all your heart, as working for the Lord, not for men, since you know that you will receive an inheritance from the Lord as a reward. It is the Lord Christ you are serving.

Colossians 3:23,24

If anyone serves, he should do it with the strength God provides, so that in all things God may be praised through Jesus Christ.

1 Peter 4:11

If they obey and serve Him, they will spend the rest of their days in prosperity and their years in contentment.

Job 36:11

God is not unjust; He will not forget your work and the love you have shown Him as you have helped His people and continue to help them.

Hebrews 6:10

"Whoever serves Me must follow Me; and where I am, My servant also will be. My Father will honor the one who serves Me."

John 12:26

GIVING THANKS & PRAISE

Give thanks to the Lord, for He is good;
His love endures forever.

Psalm 106:1

Let them give thanks to the Lord for His
unfailing love and His wonderful deeds...

Psalm 107:15

Be joyful always; pray continually; give
thanks in all circumstances, for this is
God's will for you in Christ Jesus.

1 Thessalonians 5:16-18

Therefore, since we are receiving a
kingdom that cannot be shaken, let us be
thankful, and so worship God acceptably
with reverence and awe...

Hebrews 12:28

Praise be to His glorious name forever;
may the whole earth be filled with His
glory.

Psalm 72:19

Praise the Lord. How good it is to sing praises to our God, how pleasant and fitting to praise Him!

Psalm 147:1

"My soul praises the Lord and my spirit rejoices in God my Savior, for He has been mindful of the humble state of His servant."

Luke 1:46-48

"Praise be to the Lord...because He has come and has redeemed His people."

Luke 1:68

Through Jesus, therefore, let us continually offer to God a sacrifice of praise...

Hebrews 13:15

I will give thanks to the Lord because of His righteousness and will sing praise to the name of the Lord Most High.

Psalm 7:17

Enter His gates with thanksgiving and His courts with praise; give thanks to Him and praise His name.

Psalm 100:4

FAITH

Trust in the Lord with all your heart
and lean not on your own understanding...

Proverbs 3:5

"...if you have faith as small as
a mustard seed, you can say to this
mountain, 'Move from here to there'
and it will move. Nothing will be
impossible for you."

Matthew 17:20

Now faith is being sure of what we hope
for and certain of what we do not see.

Hebrews 11:1

"Everything is possible for him who believes."

Mark 9:23

"Have faith in the Lord your God and you will be upheld..."

2 Chronicles 20:20

"...whoever lives and believes in Me will never die."

John 11:26

...take up the shield of faith, with which you can extinguish all the flaming arrows of the evil one.

Ephesians 6:16

HOPE

In His great mercy He has given us new birth into a living hope through the resurrection of Jesus Christ...

1 Peter 1:3

...those who hope in the Lord will inherit the land.

Psalm 37:9

And hope does not disappoint us, because God has poured out His love into our hearts by the Holy Spirit, whom He has given us.

Romans 5:5

...those who hope in the Lord will renew their strength. They will soar on wings like eagles...

Isaiah 40:31

And we rejoice in the hope of the glory of God.

Romans 5:2

Be strong and take heart, all you who hope in the Lord.

Psalm 31:24

The Lord is good to those whose hope is in Him, to the one who seeks Him; it is good to wait quietly for the salvation of the Lord.

Lamentations 3:25,26

COURAGE

...those who hope in the Lord will renew their strength. They will soar on wings like eagles...

Isaiah 40:31

I can do everything through Him Who gives me strength.

Philippians 4:13

"Do not let your hearts be troubled and do not be afraid."

John 14:27

"The Lord is my helper; I will not be afraid."

Hebrews 13:6

"But now I urge you to keep up your courage, because not one of you will be lost..."

Acts 27:22

The Lord is my light and my salvation—
whom shall I fear?

Psalm 27:1

Finally, be strong in the Lord and in His
mighty power.

Ephesians 6:10

For God did not give us a spirit of timidity,
but a spirit of power, of love and of self-
discipline.

2 Timothy 1:7

But perfect love drives out fear...

1 John 4:18

"So do not fear, for I am with you; do not
be dismayed, for I am your God. I will
strengthen and help you; I will uphold you
with My righteous right hand."

Isaiah 41:10

LOVE

Love is patient, love is kind...It always protects, always trusts, always hopes, always perseveres. Love never fails.

1 Corinthians 13:4,7-8

We love because He first loved us.

1 John 4:19

And now these three remain: faith, hope and love. But the greatest of these is love.

1 Corinthians 13:13

...if we love each other, God lives in us and His love is made complete in us.

1 John 4:12

And over all these virtues put on love, which binds them all together in perfect unity.

Colossians 3:14

...let us love one another, for love comes
from God.

1 John 4:7

"My command is this: Love each other as I
have loved you."

John 15:12

The entire law is summed up in a single
command: "Love your neighbor as
yourself."

Galatians 5:14

...let us not love with words or tongue but
with actions and in truth.

1 John 3:18

If I speak in the tongues of men and of
angels, but have not love, I am only a
resounding gong or a clanging cymbal.

1 Corinthians 13:1

PATIENCE

Wait for the Lord; be strong and take heart
and wait for the Lord.

Psalm 27:14

Be joyful in hope, patient in affliction,
faithful in prayer.

Romans 12:12

Be completely humble and gentle; be
patient, bearing with one another in love.

Ephesians 4:2

But the fruit of the Spirit is love, joy,
peace, patience, kindness, goodness,
faithfulness, gentleness and self-control.

Galatians 5:22,23

You need to persevere so that when you
have done the will of God, you will
receive what He has promised.

Hebrews 10:36

Perseverance must finish its work so that you may be mature and complete, not lacking anything.

James 1:4

Refrain from anger and turn from wrath; do not fret—it leads only to evil.

Psalm 37:8

A patient man has great understanding, but a quick-tempered man displays folly.

Proverbs 14:29

A gentle answer turns away wrath, but a harsh word stirs up anger.

Proverbs 15:1

The end of a matter is better than its beginning, and patience is better than pride. Do not be quickly provoked in your spirit...

Ecclesiastes 7:8

Everyone should be quick to listen, slow to speak and slow to become angry, for man's anger does not bring about the righteous life that God desires.

James 1:19,20

FORGIVENESS

Be kind and compassionate to one another, forgiving each other, just as in Christ God forgave you.

Ephesians 4:32

"For if you forgive men when they sin against you, your heavenly Father will also forgive you."

Matthew 6:14

Bear with each other and forgive whatever grievances you may have against one another. Forgive as the Lord forgave you.

Colossians 3:13

Then Peter came to Jesus and asked, "Lord, how many times shall I forgive my brother when he sins against me? Up to seven times?"

Jesus answered, "I tell you, not seven times, but seventy-seven times."

Matthew 18:21,22

"And when you stand praying, if you hold anything against anyone, forgive him, so that your Father in heaven may forgive you your sins."

Mark 11:25

Do not let the sun go down while you are still angry...

Ephesians 4:26

HUMILITY

He guides the humble in what is right and
teaches them His way.

Psalm 25:9

Pride goes before destruction, a haughty
spirit before a fall. Better to be lowly in
spirit...

Proverbs 16:18

A man's pride brings him low, but a man
of lowly spirit gains honor.

Proverbs 29:23

"This is the one I esteem: he who is
humble and contrite in spirit..."

Isaiah 66:2

"Blessed are the meek, for they will inherit
the earth."

Matthew 5:5

"Take My yoke upon you and learn from
Me, for I am gentle and humble in heart..."

Matthew 11:29

"Therefore, whoever humbles himself like this child is the greatest in the kingdom of heaven."

Matthew 18:4

"For whoever exalts himself will be humbled, and whoever humbles himself will be exalted."

Matthew 23:12

"He has brought down rulers from their thrones but has lifted up the humble."

Luke 1:52

Be completely humble and gentle; be patient, bearing with one another in love.

Ephesians 4:2

Humble yourselves before the Lord, and He will lift you up.

James 4:10

GUIDANCE

He makes me lie down in green pastures,
He leads me beside quiet waters, He
restores my soul. He guides me in paths of
righteousness for His name's sake.

Psalm 23:2,3

You guide me with Your counsel, and
afterward You will take me into glory.

Psalm 73:24

Your statutes are my delight; they are my
counselors.

Psalm 119:24

Your word is a lamp to my feet and a light
for my path.

Psalm 119:105

If I rise on the wings of the dawn, if I settle on
the far side of the sea, even there Your
hand will guide me...

Psalm 139:9,10

Whether you turn to the right or to the left, your ears will hear a voice behind you, saying, "This is the way; walk in it."

Isaiah 30:21

"The Lord will guide you always..."

Isaiah 58:11

"...the rising sun will come to us from heaven to shine on those living in darkness and in the shadow of death, to guide our feet into the path of peace."

Luke 1:78,79

When Jesus spoke again to the people, He said, "I am the light of the world. Whoever follows Me will never walk in darkness, but will have the light of life."

John 8:12

Jesus answered, "I am the way and the truth and the life."

John 14:6

"But when He, the Spirit of truth, comes, He will guide you into all truth."

John 16:13

The fear of the Lord is the beginning of wisdom, and knowledge of the Holy One is understanding.

Proverbs 9:10

Who is wise and understanding among you? Let him show it by his good life, by deeds done in the humility that comes from wisdom.

James 3:13

But the wisdom that comes from heaven is first of all pure; then peace-loving, considerate, submissive, full of mercy and good fruit, impartial and sincere.

James 3:17

For the Lord gives wisdom, and from His mouth come knowledge and understanding.

Proverbs 2:6

Trust in the Lord with all your heart and lean not on your own understanding...

Proverbs 3:5

If any of you lacks wisdom, he should ask God, Who gives generously to all without finding fault, and it will be given to him.

James 1:5

We know also that the Son of God has come and has given us understanding, so that we may know Him Who is true.

1 John 5:20

"Ask and it will be given to you; seek and you will find; knock and the door will be opened to you."

Matthew 7:7

"If you hold to My teaching...you will know the truth, and the truth will set you free."

John 8:31,32

COMFORT

The Lord is my shepherd, I shall lack nothing. He makes me lie down in green pastures, He leads me beside quiet waters, He restores my soul.

Even though I walk through the valley of the shadow of death, I will fear no evil, for You are with me; Your rod and Your staff, they comfort me.

Psalm 23:1-4

The righteous cry out, and the Lord hears them; He delivers them from all their troubles. The Lord is close to the broken-hearted and saves those who are crushed in spirit.

Psalm 34:17,18

God is our refuge and our strength, an ever present help in trouble.

Psalm 46:1

Cast your cares on the Lord and He will sustain you; He will never let the righteous fall.

Psalm 55:22

He heals the brokenhearted and binds up their wounds.

Psalm 147:3

So do not fear, for I am with you; do not be dismayed for I am your God. I will strengthen and help you...

Isaiah 41:10

For the Lord comforts His people and will have compassion on His afflicted ones.

Isaiah 49:13

The Lord is good, a refuge in times of trouble. He cares for those who trust in Him...

Nahum 1:7

"Come to Me, all you who are weary and burdened, and I will give you rest."

Matthew 11:28

"Do not let your hearts be troubled. Trust in God; trust also in Me."

John 14:1

Praise be to the God and Father of our Lord Jesus Christ, the Father of compassion and the God of all comfort, Who comforts us in all our troubles, so that we can comfort those in any trouble with the comfort we ourselves have received from God.

2 Corinthians 1:3,4

Cast all your anxiety on Him because He cares for you.

1 Peter 5:7

And we know that in all things God works for the good of those who love Him, who have been called according to His purpose.

Romans 8:28

...do not be surprised at the painful trial you are suffering, as though something strange were happening to you. But rejoice that you participate in the sufferings of Christ, so that you may be overjoyed when His glory is revealed.

1 Peter 4:12,13

...weeping may remain for a night, but rejoicing comes in the morning.

Psalm 30:5

"Blessed are those who mourn, for they will be comforted."

Matthew 5:4

For I am convinced that neither death nor life...will be able to separate us from the love of God that is in Christ Jesus our Lord.

Romans 8:38,39

He will wipe away every tear from their eyes. There will be no more death or mourning or crying or pain...

Revelation 21:4

PRAYER

"...whatever you ask for in prayer, believe that you have received it, and it will be yours."

Mark 11:24

"Ask and it will be given to you; seek and you will find; knock and the door will be opened to you."

Matthew 7:7

I love the Lord for He heard my voice...Because He turned His ear to me, I will call on Him as long as I live.

Psalm 116:1,2

"You may ask Me for anything in My name, and I will do it."

John 14:14

...by prayer and petition, with thanks-giving, present your requests to God.

Philippians 4:6

Be joyful always; pray continually; give thanks in all circumstances...

1 Thessalonians 5:16-18

...pray for each other so that you may be healed. The prayer of a righteous man is powerful and effective.

James 5:16

TEMPTATION

I have hidden Your word in my heart that I might not sin against You.

Psalm 119:11

"Watch and pray so that you will not fall into temptation. The spirit is willing, but the body is weak."

Matthew 26:41

...if someone is caught in a sin, you who are spiritual should restore him gently. But watch yourself, or you also may be tempted.

Galatians 6:1

Finally, be strong in the Lord and in His mighty power. Put on the full armor of God so that you can take your stand against the devil's schemes.

Ephesians 6:10,11

...take up the shield of faith, with which you can extinguish all the flaming arrows of the evil one.

Ephesians 6:16

When tempted, no one should say, "God is tempting me." For God cannot be tempted by evil, nor does He tempt anyone...

James 1:13

Submit yourselves, then, to God. Resist the devil, and he will flee from you.

James 4:7

Be self-controlled and alert. Your enemy the devil prowls around like a roaring lion looking for someone to devour. Resist him, standing firm in the faith, because you know that your brothers throughout the world are undergoing the same kind of sufferings.

1 Peter 5:8,9

For sin shall not be your master, because you are not under law, but under grace.

Romans 6:14

So, if you think you are standing firm, be careful that you don't fall! No temptation has seized you except what is common to man. And God is faithful; He will not let you be tempted beyond what you can bear. But when you are tempted, He will also provide a way out so that you can stand up under it.

1 Corinthians 10:12,13

Because He Himself suffered when He was tempted, He is able to help those who are being tempted.

Hebrews 2:18

Let us then approach the throne of grace with confidence, so that we may receive mercy and find grace to help us in our time of need.

Hebrews 4:16

Consider it pure joy, my brothers, when-
ever you face trials of many kinds, because
you know that the testing of your faith
develops perseverance.

James 1:2,3

Blessed is the man who perseveres under
trial, because when he has stood the test, he
will receive the crown of life that God has
promised to those who love Him.

James 1:12

...you may have had to suffer grief in all
kinds of trials. These have come so that
your faith...may be proved genuine and
may result in praise, glory, and honor when
Jesus Christ is revealed.

1 Peter 1:6,7

PEACE

"Blessed are the peacemakers, for they will be called sons of God."

Matthew 5:9

"Peace I leave with you; My peace I give you."

John 14:27

Aim for perfection, listen to my appeal, be of one mind, live in peace. And the God of love and peace will be with you.

2 Corinthians 13:11

And the peace of God, which transcends all understanding, will guard your hearts and your minds in Christ Jesus.

Philippians 4:7

Let the peace of Christ rule in your hearts, since as members of one body you were called to peace.

Colossians 3:15

Jacket photograph by Richard Stacks
Scripture compiled by Jill Wolf

*Note: All Scripture is taken from the
New International Version of the Bible*